S

The Sleepwalkers

ALSO BY WILL STONE

POETRY

Glaciation – Shearsman Books (2015; 1st edition,

Salt Publishing, 2007)

Drawing in Ash – Shearsman Books (2015; 1st edition,

Salt Publishing, 2011)

TRANSLATIONS

Les Chimères – Gérard de Nerval – Menard Press (1999)

To The Silenced – Selected Poems of Georg Trakl – Arc Publications (2005)

Journeys – Stefan Zweig – Hesperus Press (2010)

Rilke in Paris – Rainer Maria Rilke & Maurice Betz

– Hesperus Press (2012)

Selected Poems of Emile Verhaeren – Arc Publications (2013)

Nietzsche – Stefan Zweig – Hesperus Press (2013)

On the End of the World – Joseph Roth – Hesperus Press (2014)

Montaigne – Stefan Zweig – Pushkin Press (2015)

Messages from a Lost World – Stefan Zweig – Pushkin Press (2016)

Will Stone

The Sleepwalkers

Shearsman Books

First published in the United Kingdom in 2016 by
Shearsman Books
50 Westons Hill Drive
Emersons Green
BRISTOL
BS16 7DF

Shearsman Books Ltd Registered Office
30–31 St. James Place, Mangotsfield, Bristol BS16 9JB
(this address not for correspondence)

www.shearsman.com

ISBN 978-1-84861-472-7

ACKNOWLEDGEMENTS
I wish to thank the following publications in which certain of these
poems appeared before they found their way into the community
of *The Sleepwalkers* :
*Agenda, The Dark Horse, The Wolf, Poetry Salzburg, The Black Herald,
Epignosis, Undertow, The Edinburgh Review* and *The Irish Times.*

I would also like to show gratitude to the following individuals who
have supported my poetic endeavours —
in Belgium: Michael Vandebril, Sven Peeters, Benno Barnard
and especially Anette van de Wiele;
elsewhere: Emma Mountcastle, Paul Stubbs, Blandine Longre,
Stephen Romer, Richie McCaffrey, Kathryn Maris, Bridget Strevens,
Patricia McCarthy, Nigel Parke, Agnes Cserhati, Michael Rattigan,
Darran Anderson, Alyson Hallett, Timothy Adès, Rosa Richardson,
Paul North, Paul Newland, Pandora Kennedy
and my cherished parents.

But paradise is locked and bolted...
We must make a journey around the world
to see if a back door has perhaps been left open.

Kleist

Contents

III

For my parents, the loved ones…

I

You walk upon corpses, beauty, undismayed…

Baudelaire

The Sea off De Haan

Silent now in darkness
are the marram grasses.
With stillness as sustenance
only the cicadas sound.
The black sea moves blindly,
a body turns, awakens slowly
like something beginning to burn.
Always the precipice, the abyss
always the curling lip of the falls,
always the mind seen slipping away.
Solitary walkers on the silver shore,
a dog shape that cavorts, lovers
forced apart by the moon's
strengthening blade of bone.
Out there patrols the immensity
with its sheathed claw of beauty.
Have no fear child to come.
A place is held in dawn's aquarium
for our last ripple, our final
tail fin twist.

Balloon Ride

Silent and smoothly darkened
pass the baskets, with the strange
reluctance of evening doves.
A last flight swept by flame roars,
space seen and space missed for
the beautiful sadness of the balloon
signing God's acre, the ochre wheat
and shadow on the foliage as it drifts
westwards then east, closer or away
like the riders' lives dangling beneath,
charcoal to the moon's chalk smudge
and thin cries that fell to our garden
and lay on the table like browning petals.
Conjured from day's offcuts, the newly
enchanted passed over us, somehow
maintaining their footing on death's
loosening scree.

The Bear of Bern

It's a perfect circle
compass-measured by man,
where the bear lives.
Concrete is the lip of the pit
over which the freshly enthralled
fling their nuggets of fruit,
so he might catch them in mid air,
standing up like a seal for a ball
swaying on his henge hindquarters,
power still, but theatrical, vulnerable
a half-naked general no one believes in,
waiting for his uniform.

The bear is beckoning down
the harvest of shrieks and gasps,
the reviving burst of juice
as his crone tooth works the fruit,
then all this repeats,
shadowing the sadness of a wave
against the dark sea wall.
The young mothers grip their infants,
rest them on the balustrade
above the bear's great half-senile head,
so they kick their feet, mewl and drool
as his giant paw pads slap the wall
then like collapsing soil, he falls
and with blunt claw scratches
the floor for errant raisins.

Now he's up again, and the growth
on his neck swings like a leather pouch

and he leans like an old tree
weighing its chances in the first
scout breezes of an oncoming storm.
Then suddenly he sits down, head up,
noble as a dusk-combed mountain.
But they do not see, nor do they feel
how deep this pit, how long the fruit
takes to fall…

The pitted muzzle sweeps testily
from side to side, the eyes they thought
lifted from a fairy-tale turn a deeper black,
disappear abruptly into the boulder head,
a pride glimpsed, power half drawn,
then a great weariness, he slumps down
the blade remains sheathed, the raisins fall.

The Sleepwalkers

For one last night of song
they ascended the sacred hill
where, like a vessel waiting to sail
over black woods and ochre fields
that immense inverted crypt of stone,
the Madeleine, swallowed them all.
Till dawn their burly wave bore down
and eddies of chant lapped at the door.
They sang unwearying, and in the houses,
sleepless, they cursed.
At dawn the singing mass spilled
onto the grey rose tinged square.
Invalids they pushed in barrows
and the mad, with colours of all nations
like feathers in their hair. They sang on,
faces flushed with conviction
and began their descent
down the dark pipe of silent villagers,
incandescent faith, unstoppable
the lava forged its course
and the square was empty but for
a speechless sun and the abbey
now held by the air alone, like
a honeycomb released of its worker load.
The double doors swung closed
and the monks furtively returned
like svelte swallows to a cliff,
from the alleys and tortuous lanes
they darted in their dark grey robes,
while the Ursuline sisters tiptoed
through their secret tunnel

beneath the road and emerged
on the lofty terraces of their Eden.

Years passed, then decades
and the white dust road
did not darken. Some said
they heard song in the distance
and the foreigners had returned.
But no one came and time
ground the event into grains that
slipped through the grates of even
the keenest memories.
Then war and furious men
came with hammers and axes to
relieve the angels of their smiling faces.
The abbey was abandoned and lay
in ruins. A century passed.
Only doves broke the silence
rustling around the cloven heads of saints
and excited swifts left their imprint on
the stonework of the tower.
The village beneath survived
and there was death and new life, love, guilt
envy and power and there was sloth.
In this warren of ever sprouting pulses
a new breed slowly shaped,
born without the memory of song
and in time they spread their kind
through all the neighbouring lands.
Plague did not finish them
and neither did the floods, they endured
melting ice, storms and quakes
they just kept coming back, stronger
like a willingly beheaded plant.
So successful was their wisdom that

today there is no more room for them.
They point vaguely to other planets
and sigh for the lost knowledge of
how to sing together.
For every evil, they blame each other,
on how to go forwards or back
they cannot agree, or decisively act
for they have still not woken, and
will never wake from their delicious
and diverting slumber, this race
named beyond their sight, by
those who must soon step in, as
The Sleepwalkers.

A Brussels Park at Winter's End

After the drawn out winter, the sun
ordered people back into the park.
Swans applied make up to the plain pond
and a few on benches opened books
watched by an armed guard of dreams.
The peacock tossed its tasselled head
and a child overcome by the smoke
of its birth careered into the mesh.
A few climbers suddenly appeared
on the summit of a certain happiness.
Two donkeys in an enclosure
stood side by side, so still, their eyes
dark wells where the moon
will later stoop to drink its fill.
Watch the little ones leap the low fence
and run through the blown litter of doves,
maypole dancing their curiosity
around the burbling aviary,
their questioning frowns answered
by each downy eruption.

Return to Covehithe

The dead end – the drop
where tarmac shears off
the old lane still going East,
a horse at the knacker's rearing in terror,
heavy with its past, still confused
by the reminiscence of riders.
Last stop for all is the flinty ruin
but bramble patrols now bar the way in,
the fresh cliff path, down on the beach,
in car sized chunks, the plucky turf
grotesquely scattered like torn off wigs.
Three grey geese in flight, so low,
needle their thread through the fog.
The beautiful way they vanish
above the soft auburn destruction,
their black wing beats like cowls
turned to the wind, empty nests
slowly drawn over the creamy combine
of the falls.

Before the Storm Wave

Written in Hawker's Hut on the coast of North Cornwall

In early spring
you emerge from the land,
like a tiny flame's unsure birth
to stand before the storm wave,
the white wall of windblown oaks
that carries the missing aloft,
then blunders into the sand's burial,
the incoherent speech of the rock.
Muscling streams run off the land
unable to resist their own motion,
eager to shatter their dark crystal
on the bay of pebbles, they bow
their heads and slip from the gully
into the black boom of the cove,
where the undertow paws and prowls
and gulls raise up the air's scalp
through the primeval roar
of the shale.

The Singer

Her voice is
black ice forming
and when the note is held
she is slender, a wind-heaved poplar,
a dark vase with one pale flower
about to drop its last petal
on the blue lips of the dead.
Her body is the corollary
no one dares touch.
She is all the time left to us,
suddenly declaring itself at once.
Her voice is candlelight
feeling over brickwork
in the deepest wells,
she is the one to follow,
drawing us out like poison
from the last deep excavation.

London 2015

The great spit turns…
All knives are easily slicing
in the gaudy Chinese quarter,
the latest Russians and Albanians
sweep out the spent chimeras.
Pleadings of the homeless Romanian,
but the purring cash dispenser
has a healthier heart, lit by the gaze
of distant men who set the snares,
till dawn's bloody finger finds
the last good vein of the earth.
Men pass through bruised parks
darkly leaved and dressed with
lime blossom and spent needles,
for all converge on the late night show
of a crouched and feral moon.
A night of shame or delirious hope
has been forecast.
The haunted and hungry wrap up
in what's left of burned out stars.

By the Serpentine

The bearing down of black cab snout,
along Rotten Row where wet amber
circles past dark portcullis trunks.
Deeper in, a sheen of fowl push
their peeping past a terrace,
where the undone sigh, sift and sort
and weakly cast their lines of command
to deaf damp dogs.
And nothing more is heard.
Then the great city's shale sounds,
and they come, elderly actor
with young admirer, lady
from the fashion house and a few
scarlet old soldiers puffing through.
Traffic steams open the bridge.
Dark headed ducks bill-pepper
the black secret of the surface
that guards what's drowned,
a doll's torso, bare tree crowns.
Your own footfall on the wet path
was left out of the inventory,
only the gull's cry was recorded
suddenly ripping through the mist,
siren for the slowly waking survivors
resting against the reclining nude
of the pond.

The Wood by the Sea

Out of dark pines and scented glades
wakening from the weight of warm deer,
onto the track with its grassy spine
running between bulging hedgerows
that shoot out finches and sparrows.
Murmuring Eden
you go down between them, drawn
to the blue back rise of the German ocean.
Here is the meadow, ante-room
to the shadow emporium.
Solitude delivers sermons
deep in the wood whose seaward trees
share the exhaustion of migrating birds,
or drink the smoke purer than air
from the burning of fulfilled leaves.
Find me in the wood by the sea,
sprawled amidst the spirit ingredients,
shorn of the eternal human madness
in the judgement drone of bees.
The surf turns differently at dusk,
the first owl sounds, and the moon
emerges obediently above us.
Reeds, grasses whisper anchorage,
as the light fails, their tenderness enfolds
the narrow limbs of the darkening mere.

Work in Progress

The artist has left a dark cloth
draped over the unfinished canvas.
The angel who stayed behind to see
has passed now into silence.
On the melancholy smugglers' path
the solitary walker hugs the estuary,
obeying the command of black inlets.
At dusk the roe deer finds a roost
in the copse of tiny oaks.
The breeze leads us through the boughs,
we struggle down the bramble slope,
to the reeds, waves of unearthed bone
under a lowering lavender sky.
You turn back before the great bend,
the lights curl open like flowers
in the windows of distant houses.
In the cathedral of the marshes,
the nave is a heavy block of darkness.
No longer are the candles in the side chapels
lit before Vespers by the silent nun
who held the saint's yellowed rib bone
tied with a silk ribbon to her heart.

The Return

In the end the answer does not come,
there are gulls below us and leaping ferns
Evening smokes them out from the timber womb
the haven formed of dead ships' bones,
and the Atlantic, a gown thrown down by a god
who keeps for himself the vanishing bridges of gold.
Sprites of light fuss around those dark attendants
the waves, as the last disk embers whisper,
'be sure to look after the moon,' and we obey,
climb the high slate steps through the furze,
our vanishing catching on emerging stars.

Le Chateau de Valgençeuse

Memories of the Valois

Lost domain, air pocket, happy fault in the loom,
gift given only when death's back is turned.
You enter and are the only one to breathe
the mist-seasoned avenues of yew,
soil fragrant urns and perfectly weighted pools.
Ferns, their juvenile green forcing speech
from unworldly stone, naiads' voices
smoked out by the Nonette's slow turns.
On the lake's slender arm, dark dragonflies
repair the nets of surface shadow.
A plash and a plop, the otter's frozen muscle.
Just for a moment, our eyes are one,
then mine suddenly left, the game abandoned,
the surface quickly remade, never broken.
Between the anchor roots of the island
and over slippery hooped bridges of iron,
to the carcass of the summerhouse
where in mossy silence poets brushed past
and now a grey fox springs, nailed to a board
unblinking for eternity, preserved in fear.
But visitors dismantle the dream,
one by one they come as if requested
to endorse your draining away.
At the gates a concealed lord looms.
'Monsieur, c'est vous qui avez traduit
notre grand poète Gérard de Nerval?'
Yes Sir and I believe he once carried
from here a bulging sack of hope,
until beside the Acheron they laid him out.

La Chartreuse – Villeneuve-lès-Avignon

Cistercians they were,
but the brothers no longer walk here
dripping holy water, shedding ash flakes
and seeds from the dying copse fires.
The perfume of wax and lavender has gone.
No more unnecessary movements of faith
under the open vault, the chance collapse
that sometimes snows stars.

Monks themselves attacked the capitals,
their flushed faces just out of reach
of a winged beast's revengeful claw.
Dust and mortar settled, then prayer,
in cells now centrally heated, where
dramatists toil, touching all but stone,
all that that can never be warmed
by breath, blood or sacrifice, nor by belief
handed down so naturally, naively.

Corners of cloister voids easily turned,
where the sighs of robes once lingered,
where there was pain and it was meant for
tracing shapes no one now understands.
Those who came afterwards, who felt
the dark cypress shape and the war tower,
placed their faces in an arrow slit
to search the plain where no pennants fly
no swaying palisades of spears, no weary cries
over the beard growth of war, a prince's duties.

All just fell away, leaving the fortress,
the levelled water, the sky throwing back a glance,
framing reed columns,
stiffened, banner high in winter sun,
trusting the too wide Rhone
from whose grey blue muscular body, even now,
every mortal gaze slips defeated.

Old Outhouse

Fig leaf shadows flicker strangely
on the dirty white-washed walls.
Web hammocks swing gently
in the single lancet cell.
Perfume of oil spilt long ago,
broken pots collapsed, abandoned
beside their clay blood trail.
The wind, tireless, works at a hole
and resigned now to oblivion
the noble silence of obsolete tools.
On a shelf the rust outline
of long departed nails, the stiffened
corpse of a gardening glove, and
higher up a brush filled tea cup,
seized paint tins behind which
a queen wasp privately expires.
As you kick the stuck door, in welcome
excited spiders race up and down
the worn stairs of their webs.

Zurich

Cold women made colder by furs.
The bearing down of buffed blue
and white trams.
All footage of insanity confiscated.
Surveillance under surveillance.
The gentrified cobbled lanes, frets
of the old town disappearing,
globalised, googled, glazed.
Only the swans seem untouched,
billowing like the skirts of leaping
suicides over the ebony waters
beneath *Fraumünster* at dusk.

Night Spider

All day he waited, then
when the sun's speech ended
he dangled out, swung like a drunk
still attached by one claw
to the tavern door.
All night he had endured the rain.
To him distant thunder is a feeling,
the welling of a tiny drop
of his own black blood, the wind
a chance to tense, to quiver, then fail
like a lonely face at a window
refused by the laughter inside.
With his swag he returns to the hole,
and the darkness reforms him.
He remains unseen and unread
poised, alert, without knowing why,
eyeing life's brilliant white bone.

The Sleepwalkers II

The child stepped forward from the choir
his human face resisting the ruffed angelic,
the child of today framed in the most sublime
transition from Romanesque to Gothic
and then he began his solo and the voice
simply stepped out from his soul, hung there
and was stolen by swifts that wheeled in
from the narthex through the wide open doors.
These couriers held it aloft near the capitals
where the mythological creatures are
and it was sustained beyond the grasping
upward claw of reality, above the ears of men
who, scattered in the nave, struggled to bring
it down and hold it to their hearts.
Then the applause came and the lonely fire
was kicked out. But where smoke still hung,
that brief moment clung on and refused
to fall back into the embers and be interred.
Then the great abbey bell began to toll
and the lit fuse ran to the other churches,
for a single un-sacred child had fed them all
and with his beautiful life,
not faith, angel apparition or miracle,
reversed the certainty of another century
of darkness.

II

Posterity will not be able to understand that we had to fall back into the same darkness after having known the light...

Castellion

Reading Reck

In Memory of Friedrich Reck-Malleczewen (1884-1945)

Genickschuss – a bullet in the neck
improvised methods improved,
the cause inked into the columns
as he slept, the black pack ice drifted in
and finally reached Friedrich Reck.
One of the last, he whittled an existence
on the reducing floe, Reck in his wood
glancing around him, a silhouette
with his hands in the earth, digging,
as the creatures looked on, the light failed.
Reck, who found a fawn torn by a dog
and cradled it as it died, 'with tears in its eyes'
fraught with confusion and then
Reck remembered the laughing whaler,
the mother, trying in her bloody throes
to protect her doomed infant.
Every night he interred his growing offspring,
the makeshift shelter against insanity
under which he crouched, sending language
past the indifferent eyes of owls,
or struggled into Munich on stinking trams
his head swaying amongst the dolls,
fighting his way through the hollow men
to our time where the remains were scattered
and disguised as something else.
All the useless forms that passed his cell,
the dark eddies competing behind the dam
and Reck pacing, drawn down,
as the sand timer bows to the thirst
of the sand to build its glitter dune.

No one comes, only once the sun forced
its tiny pale hand through the grille.
Sprawled on the shingle of prayer
the future finds him, a last flare
then everything stops.

The Gang's All Here

The happy date drew near.
They checked a fresh team
was on hand to replace them,
set off for the site of relaxation.
Sleepy following the welcome feast
the accordion player roused them,
had them pose for a snapshot
above the rustic bridge of boughs.
They assembled awkwardly
the off duty gentlemen, stiffly ranked
like an amateur male choir
in the club uniform.
Their mouths involuntarily open
because the brass on the bridge
urges them on, for the team song.
Cigars for the bosses, the sharing
of managerial gossip, a bawdy joke.
Refreshment sustains the glowing
filament of shared conviction.
Time to unwind, time away at last
from the tired gait of the shop floor,
the dull assemblage of materials,
recycling and sensible exploitation
of the offcuts that litter the yard
day in day out, a welcome break
from eleventh hour improvisation,
from the sudden roving inspection,
the pressure to meet targets.
Giggling typists and telephonists
look flirtatiously on from a sunny glade.
Some whistle, some wave, they are

just doing what comes naturally,
for they are young people with dreams
riding their float through the carnival,
lips stained with the blood
of blueberries.

Treblinka Zoo

The final storm has not yet passed
and the air hangs uncertain in the ark.
They lead them out, the exotic beasts
strike their rumps and shout *'Raus!'*
And the upward flame that reflected
in their eyes offered the future its frost.

Flower meadows bloomed there,
because they were sown and watered
where farmers squabbled long after,
crows, beak stabbing for coins and jewels
how easily they tore through a million souls
as greed calmly reset its rifle sights
and the elders blew open the graves.

Between here and the Black Road
they built the zoo, those men assigned
set to work on park and menagerie,
awash with ideas, ripe with creativity.
It took them a week on and off
during pauses in their other tasks.
On the roof cooed the lucky doves
and stripped branches of silver birch
formed an ornamental balustrade.

They trawled the surrounding forest
for exotic beasts, creatures were led
into dark compartments, and sank
nervously on fresh sawdust. Some had straw.
Unprepared inmates of the enclosure
confused performers yoked for diversion,

their amber eyes followed the keepers
as they set down each feeding bowl.

They heard the practice drill, the unrolling
wire of laughter, the loco whistle to them
was a repeated danger call from a stranger.
Someone looked after teeth, hooves and fur,
someone held the gaze of the deer in dim light
and with a rush, the empty trough was filled.

On fine days the keepers touched glasses
at rustic tables arranged out front.
Each formed a relationship with an exhibit
and sometimes took them special food.
The zoo was meant for idleness, relaxation,
and in the bakery they bought their bread.

Then came a different day, roars and flames
taut chains and glistening ropes, yelling
of passing men, terror, sweat and stampede,
a dash for the forest away from the heat
and a return to the old lust for hiding.
Then gazing back at the burning, blinking
at the clearing, where they planted lupins,
where now archaeologists dig with trowels
and gamely hold up muddy combs.

Cripple King

After the load was processed
the ramp was all but deserted,
save for a single wicker chair
in which the cripple was placed.
A young man with dark eyes
a leftover piece, *ein Stück.*
One too many to be swung on
the grey truck that lurched off.
So he must wait here awhile,
driftwood after the laughter,
debris swept to the edge of
the shop floor, the monarch
patient on his wicker throne,
securely bound in the trusses
of the dust of their leaving.
He sees only the silver grey
of the poplar stream, the screen
sewn in order to hide him.
He shifts a little, the chair creaks,
born of blood, he still hopes,
accepts the advice of the sun.
How long he remained there
delayed on that wicker island,
there is no record.
But the workers returned
for what fell from the load,
quickly, like dustmen with bins
they lifted him chair and all
and being a king, bore him
aloft to join his waiting people
past the future's white face,

the strewn possessions
of centuries.

The Collector

What was not discarded
he held up, turned to the light,
the last secreted gemstones
freshly unearthed, in this place
nothing was besmirched.
Sapphire, turquoise, emerald, amber
he arranged them all so carefully,
judiciously, so beautiful he sighed
standing back to judge, to reassure,
like a painter, the collector.
No red admiral, splayed stag beetle
or dark chocolate moth,
but incarcerated with them, lost
bobbing in the jaundiced foam
of history's exhausted wave,
a medieval child's flattened shoe.
And when the work was done
he dipped his white fingers
into the jewels, calmly set aside
the accusing face, for his victory
was their gaze, their permanent
drama of impotence behind glass.
But when the wild men of the east
burst in, bringing a flurry of snow
they met not him, but the gaze.
They called for the major
and all stood in line, rooted,
silently lowering their hands
to strangle a still kicking god.
Some counted the colours
peering close as at hieroglyphs,

because they were once farm boys,
raw students of life, interred alive
they still felt behind the scream
to touch what was human.

Morning Ride

The commandant's white horse is a vessel
navigating the dark waters of the copse.
The commandant's white horse leaves
a wash of waist-high yellow grass.
The commandant's white horse expects
spur, the chatter of whip and rein...
even the embalmed pat of a gloved hand.
The commandant's countenance shows
his wife's last metronome wave
and his leather boots grow softer in the sun
that can make infernal his fiefdom,
his Eden, his exercise yard of conviction.
The commandant sits erect in the saddle
and trots past the latest excavations.
Much has been achieved since his last
pride-infected rush of blood dimmed,
when he savaged his scheming subordinates
in the hot wood interior, left them burned,
these loving fathers willing to stay sane.
The commandant's white horse and rider
emerge through insect bliss together,
marinated with fate, patrolling even now
the silver strewn wilderness, there
where the lone crow of history
chooses not to land.

Field Report

Always in an orderly manner
under difficult circumstances,
but with honourable decorum
my men carried out the operation.

Exacting duties were fulfilled with
the utmost scrupulousness.
I was concerned for their health
so ensured my men were rested.

Recognising the vital importance
of these demanding tasks
we were determined, whatever the rank,
to finish our labours by dusk.

With military precision and always
in the most humane manner
we properly executed our solemn duty.

I can hereby state categorically
from the first to the last of all my men
every one was praiseworthy.

And New Life Blooms from the Ruins

After the painting by Otto Dix, 1946

Sleepers, in the Dresden cellars
and the broad fountain bowls
brimful with black figures.
A songbird lands on a charred maple,
and then it all happens again.
Language makes emergency repairs
sense forages, bottles the grey light
from the parachute's billowing silk.
The excavator is decommissioned
and the innocuous farm installed.
The Ukrainians who stood on the jaws
have been reabsorbed into the crowd
and would prefer not to speak of the past.

Beneath the expert coldness of stars
in nests of rubble the unfed women
hitch their skirts, or in candlelight
suddenly sink their exhausted heads
onto the keys of a salvaged piano.
Sonatas and other choice leftovers
are folded carefully in velvet cloth
and patiently spoons and hairclips
make their way upwards through
the draconian loneliness of the earth.
A fresh snowfall cools the ashes further
and people reappear with new faces,
they stare out from their glass houses,
the new improved stock, the screens
buzz with memorial,
it must never happen again.

III

In our corruption we see beauties unrevealed to ancient times…

Baudelaire

Fir Forest

Rising up too darkly for men,
they sow confusion in their coldness,
haul their gradient into the ravine.
Always enough space for a hanging
over the off-cuts of scattered huts,
swallowing dust, thickly painting
over the impertinent sound of saws.
Canopies are dense but seem poor,
monotonous sap and needle speech
that draws foreboding in towards you.
Bombed cathedral, gutted house,
abyss of whispers, forbidden barn
of casually blackened wounds.
Stolen bird calls sifted, counted.
A grey procession of faith
that moves on without you,
hoarder of the stream's silver
the cowbell's gold, but forbids
passage through the untrod cloister,
where only the lonely one passes,
sees sky through rents of branches,
recognises the full moon as the face
that appeared at the window,
unconsciously drawn like the rest
to the screams of a new birth.

What once was hidden will now appear

As the venomous head sprouted
on the 'civilised' body back then,
the people now known as *we*
unable to restrain the lunatic,
feel our way into downfall again.
All is synchronised,
the exact hour of our undoing
an oncoming prow in the mist.
The first sound is the owl and then
the enemy heaving at the picket fence,
that surrounds our pristine village.

The dog sniffs the icy current
beneath the door. This is a new fear
what once was hidden will now appear.
The wagons of rhetoric are on the move,
a herd strays onto tracks still grazing,
hoping elsewhere will take the worst,
praying a body identical to theirs
will soak up the bullet first.

At the lectern another rustled up
waxwork begins his speech.
Eternal recurrence spins the spider,
as the red hood of a child recedes
against the dark coal heap of the crowd.
Storm waves are below the last house,
tireless, itching for the cornerstone.
All are inside, millions to a room
they fire flares, write pressing articles,
but for Europe, our beautiful bone yard,

the last ship of culture rich centuries
has passed on.

Fire

All is prepared for your first meal...
Shrew-like the scout flame emerges,
then taken in the talons of a draught
is lifted through the kindling to trace
the last gestures of those who died unjustly.
Your silence is all the meat
stripped from the bone of a shriek,
stripped quickly by your razor teeth.
You start to grow, to seed, to seek
and your eyes stare wildly
through the died-back foliage of history.
You thrust your face towards the sun's,
shooting black leaf upwards
to unsettle the pride of a blue sky.

The genie of sparks, the cherub flame
your foot soldiers are always seen
sprinting away with the colours.
In the pocket of life, in the pay of death
you wolf leap onto a trussed heretic,
prise a priest from his hole, conjure to ash
the child who hid in the confession box.
You turn a mass grave into a benign copse,
leaving flower meadows that will bloom.
So gently you play with the child's eyes,
reward a trusting face at the hearth
then settle like a cat and blink.

You fool them all and everything alive
must eventually cross your path.
I have never known you not to perform,

to play with your prey, whip crack the air.
Then suddenly you are gone
and only a warm wind is left to dress
the carbonised stumps, the gutted hall.
New plants push through, and you
are drowning in the shallows,
bled white in the fire breaks,
and you die there without an heir,
where firs now jostle their dark prows
and lower their sails of rain.

Welcome Visitors

Between the seasons they arrive
to measure our movements.
As evening falls and the great river
permits the scouts of a new century
to cross, the visitors appear.
They stoop to load our darkest items,
even shouldering the wormy furniture
of deceit, and in protective suits
wade through drifts of ambition.
Whole teams in rows rake the ground
for evidence of mass murder, watched
by impassive functionaries.
Gladly they warm their bloodless hands
on the laughter rolling from a bar,
but the early blossom of compassion
will always catch them unwary.
In all weathers the newcomers toil
to untangle future dunes of hair,
tie our heroic failures in bundles so
on their return they'll know to whom
the bloodied fabric belongs.

Are they then our guardians?
Well ask them...
The snowflakes carried in on your hair
are the icy whispers of their resolve,
the down of assiduous deliberations,
the pattern of frost on the window
what they said in the dark about us.
Through the gap of winter's door
I saw them arriving once more,

they threw fresh garlands around
the necks of lunatics, blessed the mute
and worked with the fairy painters.
With terrible seriousness, they
counted the hearts of the loveless,
then those strange stewards moved off
to higher pastures, whistling
their black dogs, that ran and circled
the moving flocks of our crimes.

The Triumph of Death

After the painting by Pieter Brueghel the Elder

Language learned that seemed eternal
easily coming apart. The deepest crevasses
where for eternity steel ropes hang taut
but no one climbs down, no one comes out.
At all latitudes and in all theatres of war
fingernails deeply engrave the asylum wall.
On motorbikes they raced to the pyres,
hunters who selected girls to run like deer
through the thicket of dogs.
And then watching the student's expression
as she learns of ghetto and pogrom,
sighs and returns to playing the accordion.
And the unclaimed faces of Transport 20,
beaded with rain on the railings
of the Royal Park in Brussels.
And all those who rose under the ice
born for the human horizon, unknowing,
random faces stirred into the earth's crucible
of endlessly vying pasts. A world
gathering for the thaw and the retreating
armies of words, down there in history
where all the inspired euphemisms hide.
Recognised, they step out bearing the hidden
infection, like the tick gnawing at the bee.
In their nineties, those who slipped away,
the guilty, now handcuffed appear younger,
groomed for provincial courtrooms,
blundering, yet strangely smiling,
the ordinary men.

Raft Armada

The future lays its nets, space
sucks in the craft with men on board.
Mesmerised, they stare into the silo,
at the stored silence of the world.
While below on the ended earth, come
the red shoots of its last dancers,
and out there by the clanging buoy
the shark's eye rolls back powerfully.

How many coffins floated down the Rhone,
with corpses whose sockets held Roman coins?
How many years left for those maritime hens,
forts in the Thames estuary at Shivering Sands?

The trees conduct the wind in their leafage.
The grass runs back to us full of stories
and in the waiting room an infant smiles,
chuckles at me and no one knows when
we'll launch our shriek across mortuary tiles.
Eagles above us even now, yet we follow
the raft armada downstream, our echoes
empty pails striking the sides of wells.

Seventeen Days

Your epitaph
 'Sleep well little man...'
for barely awake
after seventeen days you died.
Gone before you relished the wing
quiver of your first wren, or watched
the hawk intimidate into action
those undecided first hours of spring.
Gone after a brief base struggle,
a plunge from the nest when
to no avail you felt the rushing air,
down to where no lost lamb bleat
could reach you, no fern's shy laughter
no damp bracken scent off Exmoor.
Interred before you saw your feet
ghost stir the sand in clear water.
No time to inhale a fistful of soil,
crumbling, almost moist, poised
to give hope and infinite good,
or steal from the Cornish graveyard
wild primrose bristling with bone roots,
filaments to be planted far from here
with the usual expectation...
'Sleep well little man...'
with your poor catch of hours
littered about you.

Pietà

After the pietà by Adriaen Isenbrandt
in the Musée National d'Histoire et d'Art in Luxembourg

Christ's head centred
then those of the mourners
gently orbiting it for eternity like moons.
Christ is a pale youth with a sketch of beard
and the hot graze from the thorns
is atrocity advancing, darkening his brow.
He leaks no surprise from his final
weariness and we see his eyes open
though the lids stay firmly closed.
Christ is the stamen
and each petal clings to the sustainer.
Each shoot lifts towards a possible sun.
Each face wants to turn heavenwards,
but each mourner looks across or down.
And the spear wound, an Eygptian eye
gazes emphatically from the livid body
they tenderly fold down.
One fleeting hand, but whose?
cups the collapsing shoulder,
one hand shaking, streaked with tears
underwrites the hypnosis of heads.
The plant is intact, seeks to grow
and what happened there amid moans
and the creak of nails retracted
is something that still sucks
the air from the lookers lungs,
leaves each human breath now
undetected, walled in
by the indecipherable.

The Ripening

Seedlings dropped into dark soil,
into the warm finger formed hole
and lying at the bottom of the well
the tiny corpse, planted where it fell.
They peered down, faces reflected
on the upward turned eyeballs,
in that marble they existed a while.
The old iron bucket would raise it,
but instead they filled the hole in,
patted down the soil with spades.
The sun patrolled, then the rain
made a sweep with its grey dogs
and nobody else came near.
Then something broke the surface,
out shot the tongue that tasted air
reserved for the dead who live.
Then came speech and fury
but none was there to receive it,
only a language, guardian of all,
the lips of the ascendant tasted,
code unknown to the crowd
of the word about to bloom.

Entertaining the Unconscious

The many too many recover from life.
Screens flicker on a billion eyes
as the iceberg suddenly breaks away
and nudges awake the ocean.
Each tries to remain on the floe,
but the many too many slide like seals
into the dark ice holes of history.
And the dead watch it all by satellite
huddled in their grave clothes, in
old air raid shelters, in musty sepulchres
and stretch out a bony claw
as they recognise themselves
as they once were, back when
they were a mighty sail filled
with the stiff breeze of events,
when they had eyes instead of empty
wells, where now only insects come
to sink their pails and draw their
brief existence.

Iceberg Nearing

The Iceberg Rose buds are in their silos
tightly sheathed in the assurance of green.
They are sensuous, muscular, calm
in their imagined uniqueness, plucky
pioneers of the cool night air
they tap at the high arched window,
flicking their broom against the Suffolk sky.
Now they grow darker at the hour
when the last blackbird flutters up,
dislodged rock, blown felt hat
furled flag prised open by the wind.
When inky cravats of cloud
swathe the embers, the dead are still
bushels of bones in a Somme copse
or a field of young barley, where
our gaze narrows against the sun,
comes to a rest with no reply
amidst a deranged fizzing of insects.
Who are we?
We who weave miraculously through
the smoking straw piles of the past,
our backdraught stirring
the chance of a last cauterising flame.
We who cannot prevent the sound
of the screaming geese of Sobibor
foiling the ersatz jazz of a Polish Starbucks.
Night and the rose foetus wrinkles tight,
honing its language, all that is held there,
to be spent in a single convulsion,
a lonely fire on the dark moor
that flares when our last dawn breaks.

Where the Airmen Are

In the old cemetery of Brussels
I found the entire Lancaster crew.
The oldest was only twenty-two.
Side by side they lie, cradled
now in the box-scented breeze,
in the slowly traversing willows of rain.
Unvisited except for the taciturn mower
and a hardy few placing wreathes
in irritable November weather.
Their mothers of English shires
all rest now too in turf-caped tombs
or in dusty urns in the honeycomb
of suburban crematoria.
But one of them, who stroked his cap
on the coffin, had asked
for words to be engraved here.
Our beloved Dennis
He believed in England
and fought to keep her free…
Mother.

Departure of the Loved Ones

Watching them both, in their beige raincoats,
obedient, measured, gentle, decent
sucked slowly through passport control.
I stare at what recedes, where future loss
must catch and hold, there
where the traffic is heavy in the heart,
where the ungovernable crowds mill, and
the lonely speaker turns dejectedly for home.
My parents in the seats I reserved for them,
my new born elderly children who
navigated the marble steps of Hotel Rubens
and are thoughtful to everyone
because this was their faith, they knew
no religion and were blessed.
Now I watch them recede in a chaos
of technology and systems, of guards
and glass and people who do not know.
They have slipped through now,
out of sight, can only imagine
the angel who refused my explanation
guarding them so tenderly
under his great wing.

Notes

The Bear of Bern

The bear pits of Bern have drawn visitors since medieval times and the bear is a local symbol found on flags, architecture and in works of art. On my first visit to Bern a decade ago, the unfortunate bears were still confined to the original deep stone pits. The ancient tradition is now maintained in more humane fashion. A modern bear sanctuary has replaced the pits, allowing the animals to roam beside the River Aare and swim in the waters.

The Sleepwalkers

Both of these poems are inspired by the mediaeval village of Vézelay in Burgundy. Famous for its striking position and historic Abbey, Vézelay was a key gathering point for Crusaders in the 12th century, including Richard the Lionheart himself. It is still a site of pilgrimage and religious festivals.

Le Chateau de Valgençeuse

This private chateau is located just outside the historic town of Senlis, north of Paris in the ancient province once known as Le Valois, now a portion of the greater region of Picardy.

La Chartreuse - Villeneuve-lès-Avignon

This mediaeval monastic complex is found at the heart of 'Villeneuve', just across the river from Avignon. The history of Villeneuve-lès-Avignon is every bit as interesting as that of Avignon, yet it attracts fewer tourists so the atmosphere and serenity of the ecclesiastical buildings survives relatively unscathed.

Reading Reck

Friedrich Reck-Malleczewen (1884-1945) was a Prussian aristocrat and novelist, who met Hitler in 1920 and reviled him from the first. Describing that first meeting, Reck wrote: "There was a feeling of dismay, as when on a train you suddenly find you are sharing a compartment with a psychotic." He described the "feeling of oppression" left after the young Hitler "preached" at length. "It was not that an unclean body had been in the room, but something else: the unclean essence of a monstrosity."

Reck opposed the rise of the Nazis, and during the war he kept a diary detailing the rigours of daily life under a dictatorship. He also recorded his growing revulsion towards the Nazi regime and his despair at the loss of the old Germany. Reck kept the diary buried at different locations on his estate as a precaution. In the vicious and paranoid aftermath of the July 1944 bomb plot against Hitler, Reck was arrested as a known dissenter. He was imprisoned in Dachau and shot in February 1945. The diary was never discovered by the Nazis, and was published in Germany after the war. A full English translation is now available in various editions as *Diary of a Man in Despair*.

The Gang's All Here

This title was taken from the caption ironically awarded to one of the photographs in the so-called 'Karl Höcker Album', owned by the Auschwitz-Birkenau Museum. This remarkable album of 116 photographs, discovered in 2006, had belonged to Höcker, a key SS officer at the camp. The images featured life for the SS personnel in the camp itself and also at a nearby rural 'retreat' named Solahütte, which provided a break for the SS from their daily duties at Birkenau. Höcker arrived at Auschwitz in May 1944 and most of his snapshots were taken over the next six months, before the camp was liberated in January 1945. During the summer and autumn of 1944, 400,000 Hungarian Jews were murdered at the camp.

The photograph in question shows a gathering of the 'top brass' including Commandant Rudolf Höss and Dr Josef Mengele. Here the consortium of killers is shown as one, the swaggering bosses in the first row and the faithful lesser executioners ranked up the slope behind them.

The poem also refers to other images, notably one showing a line of young female SS auxiliary staff, known as *Helferinnen*, perched on a rustic balcony gleefully tucking into bowls of blueberries. Karl Höcker himself presides over the fun, egging the girls on for the camera. The second image shows them holding their bowls upside down with mock sadness; now all the delicious blueberries are gone. Meanwhile, thirty kilometres away, thousands of human beings are being gassed, shot, or, when numbers of arrivals exceed capacity, thrown alive into firepits. Höcker faced justice after the war, but denied any wrongdoing, even though witnesses testified to his presence on the ramp during Selections. He made the following statement in court: "I only learned about the events in Birkenau... in the course of the time I was there... and I had nothing to do with that. I had no ability to influence these events in any way... neither did I want them, nor carry them out. I didn't hurt anybody... and neither did anyone die at Auschwitz because of me."

Höcker spent only seven years in prison and then returned to his post as cashier in a bank until he retired in 1970.

Treblinka Zoo

The Nazi death camp at Treblinka, situated fifty miles north east of Warsaw, was the site of the most intense human extermination in history. In almost total secrecy, Treblinka operated between July 1942 and October 1943, little more than a year, but in that period consumed hundreds of thousands of victims, the vast majority of them Jews.

The camp was relatively small, a fraction of the size of Auschwitz, and was formed of three distinct parts; the more remote extermination area itself, closely guarded and screened off by fences of barbed wire woven with fir branches; the reception and sorting area; then the living area for the SS and Ukrainian guards, at furthest distance from the killing process. It was in this part of the camp that the "zoo" was created, within a small park area , designated as a place of relaxation for the SS. Here Himmler's finest would unwind after their labours, bathed in the murmur of gently cooing doves. However, the Treblinka zoo was short lived. Following a desperate uprising by prisoners in August 1943, and with the majority of Poland's Jews now eliminated, the SS razed the camp in an attempt to destroy all evidence of their crimes. The land was ploughed to bare earth, planted with meadow flowers and a benign looking forester's hut installed.

Cripple King

This poem refers to a rare photograph (photographer and subject unknown) showing a disabled man with dwarfism, abandoned on the ramp at Birkenau, in the aftermath of Selection.

The Collector

The collector in question is Josef Mengele, the Auschwitz doctor who performed barbaric medical experiments on prisoners. Under the banner of rational pathology, Mengele assembled a collection of specimens from his victims.

Morning Ride

The commandant of Auschwitz, Rudolf Höss, was often seen riding around the more pastoral areas of the complex on a white horse. From his scrupulously polished saddle he would inspect his domain like some feudal Lord of the Manor, keeping an eye on his underlings and workers.

Field Report

This poem draws on the contents of an actual report made from the field by a commander of an SS *Einsatzgruppe* "cleansing" unit on the Eastern front in 1941. I have retained the actual wording as far as possible.

Where the Airmen Are

The old Brussels Cemetery at Evere is the largest and most romantic in the city, yet hardly anyone beyond Brussels even knows of its existence. Among the labyrinthine alleys, cobbled avenues and overgrown plots of this sprawling village of the dead are a number of military memorials. One of these is dedicated to fallen Allied airmen of the Second World War. Here lie lost men of England, close to where their bombers were shot down. Unlike the vast orderly ranks of the Somme, these graves are arranged in small enclosures, carefully tended amid the riotous abandon of the surrounding funerary landscape.

The Author

Will Stone, born 1966, is a poet, essayist and literary translator. His first poetry collection, *Glaciation* (Salt Publications, 2007), won the international Glen Dimplex Award for poetry in 2008. A second collection, *Drawing in Ash*, was published by Salt in 2011. Shearsman Books republished these collections in new editions in 2015, and the present volume, his third collection, completes the trilogy.

Will's published translations include *To the Silenced – Selected Poems of Georg Trakl* (Arc Publications, 2005) and *Journeys*, a collection of Stefan Zweig's European travel essays (Hesperus Press, 2010). His first English translation of *Rilke in Paris* by Maurice Betz appeared from Hesperus Press in 2012. In 2013 Hesperus published two more translations, *Nietzsche* by Stefan Zweig and *On the End of the World*, Joseph Roth's essays from his Parisian exile during the 1930s. Pushkin Press published his translation of *Montaigne* by Stefan Zweig in 2015 and then in 2016, as *Messages from a Lost World*, Zweig's poignant essays and speeches from his exile during the 1930s. Arc published his Emile Verhaeren *Poems* in 2013, the first modern translation into English of the Belgian poet's work and a second volume will appear from Arc in 2016 dedicated to the poetry of Georges Rodenbach. Seagull Books will publish his *Collected Poems of Georg Trakl* in 2017.

Will is currently writing a book on the more overlooked elements of the culture, history and landscape of Belgium. His reviews and essays have been published in a number of journals including *The Times Literary Supplement*, *The London Magazine*, *Poetry Review* and *The White Review*.